CW00742584

Turn Your Talents Into Gold

Create the business of your dreams with your
unique abilities, skills, and experience

A step-by-step guide

Debbie Barwick

Bloomington, IN   Milton Keynes, UK

AuthorHouse™
1663 Liberty Drive, Suite 200
Bloomington, IN 47403
www.authorhouse.com
Phone: 1-800-839-8640

AuthorHouse™ UK Ltd.
500 Avebury Boulevard
Central Milton Keynes, MK9 2BE
www.authorhouse.co.uk
Phone: 08001974150

The facts and suggestions contained in this book are for informational purposes only and are not meant to take the place of tax, legal or business advice. Neither the author nor publisher takes responsibility for the success or failure of any business endeavor inspired by this book.

First published by AuthorHouse 2/6/2008

ISBN: 978-1-4259-6959-2 (e)
ISBN: 978-1-4259-6958-5 (sc)

Printed in the United States of America
Bloomington, Indiana

This book is printed on acid-free paper.

Library of Congress Control Number: 2006908953

"Twenty years from now you will be more disappointed
by the things you didn't do than by the ones you did.
So throw off the bowlines. Sail away from the safe harbor.
Catch the trade winds in your sails. Explore. Dream."

Mark Twain

Dedication

This book is devoted to all true entrepreneurs who—in spite of setbacks and obstacles—forge ahead to achieve their dreams.

Table of Contents

Introduction

George Bernard Shaw once quipped, "I don't believe in circumstances. The people who get on in this world are the people who get up and look for the circumstances they want and, if they can't find them, make them." Do you want to be your own boss doing what you love to do? Then there's no better time to start than now! Creating and operating a business is certainly a challenge, but very much worth it.

This guide is designed to help you organize the basic foundation for your business, one stone at a time. In faithfully following the step-by-step assignments, you'll find that pursuing your dream is not as overwhelming as it may be if you tried to do everything at once. By pacing yourself, you'll create a sturdy enterprise that will stand the test of time.

It is strongly recommended that you read this book twice. The first time, you'll become familiar with "the big picture" and what it takes to construct and operate a company. The second time, fulfill each assignment in order and check it off as you go. You'll find that—at the end of the book—you'll have a new business, up and running!

Note: Instead of marking in the book itself, you may want to photocopy the pages with checklists and then post the pages where you can view your goals and monitor your progress on a regular basis. Also, make notes (as suggested in each chapter) on separate sheets of paper. This way you can log your accomplishments and notations and make changes, if you wish.

Don't wait...plan on success today!

The successful entrepreneur takes charge of the present, looks forward to the future, and never glances back. Picturing yourself succeeding is the first step. But don't just sit there and dream...start now by this book and completing the assignments. Best wishes to you in your new and exciting endeavor!

CHAPTER 1

Start with a Winning Attitude

"Think you can; think you can't – either way, you're right."
Henry Ford

What do you think is the most important key to a successful business? Is it start-up capital? Yes, that definitely helps. Is it taking time to "grow" your enterprise? That is also important. However, many people are unaware that the most vital investment is your **attitude**. The saying "Success begins in the mind" is absolutely true. You can achieve your dream, and don't let anyone talk you out of it. As challenges come along, turn obstacles into opportunities. Envision yourself having already achieved your heart's desire and keep persevering.

Get started
- Write down three reasons you want to start your own business (i.e., time freedom, more money, be your own boss, etc.).

1.

2.

3.

Now hold those three thoughts and concentrate on their importance to you.

Think like a millionaire!
Author Thomas J. Stanley, Ph.D., surveyed hundreds of millionaires and found that "a disproportionately high percentage of millionaires, multimillionaires, and decamillionaires are self-employed business

owners and entrepreneurs or self-employed professionals." Replying to his inquiry regarding their secrets of success, the millionaires said:

- "We think of success, not failure. We take risk but we study the probable outcomes. And we do everything we can to enhance the odds of generating returns."

- "How do we eliminate or reduce fear and worry and bolster our courage? We practice believing in ourselves and hard work."

- "How do we bolster our belief in ourselves? We focus on key issues; we prepare and plan to succeed; and we are well organized to deal with big issues."

- "Nearly four in ten (37 percent) of us reduce the fears and worries associated with making critical decisions about financial resources in another way—we call upon our strong religious faith. In fact, those among us who have strong religious faith have a higher propensity to take financial risk than others."

The Millionaire Mind. Thomas J. Stanley, Ph.D. Andrews McMeel Publishing, 2001.

Think positive thoughts and associate with positive people

To keep motivated, read uplifting materials and associate with positive people. Don't let anyone talk you out of your goals. Napoleon Hill, author of the timeless classic *Think & Grow Rich* explains that persistence is one of the great attributes of success and states "…four simple steps lead to the habit of persistence. They call for no great amount of intelligence, no particular amount of education, and but little time or effort."

He states that "The necessary steps are:

- A definite purpose backed by burning desire for its fulfillment.

- A definite plan expressed in continuous action.

- A mind closed tightly against all negative and discouraging influences.

- A friendly alliance with one or more persons who will encourage one to follow through with both plan and purpose."

Tap into the power of prayer

I would like to say a word about the power of prayer and meditation. I'm sure that somewhere along the path to creating your own business, as well as other worthwhile endeavors in your life, there have been— and will be—times of abject discouragement and depression. Consider evaluating your hopes and dreams, then asking for guidance from a higher source.

Positive affirmations

Mike Brescia, president of a positive thinking organization (www. thinkrightnow.com) shares his thoughts about the techniques Jeff Gross, a mortgage consultant from California, used to win a substantial sum of money on the popular show *Who Wants to be a Millionaire*? "Jeff said that after he found out he was going to be on the show, he began doing daily mantras (affirmations). As often as he possibly could, he would repeat three statements to himself. He would also look in the mirror and repeat them out loud with emotion. Here's what he said:

- I am going to answer all 15 questions correctly.

- I am going to win a million dollars.

- I am going to be the best contestant *Millionaire* has ever had.

"He was a gutsy player, not using lifelines even when he wasn't quite sure of an answer. After he correctly guessed the $100,000 question, the host said she couldn't tell if he was incredibly foolish or incredibly brilliant. Forward he marched. He went against what the audience majority told him to do on the $250,000 question and he was right.

"After correctly answering/guessing 14 questions in a row, he got to the million dollar question…and he didn't know the answer. So without any lifelines left, he wisely took the money -- $500,000 (half a million)."

Post these affirmations where you can see them and repeat them to yourself as you look in the mirror. Affirmations work! As you can see, the mind is a powerful tool to help you achieve your goals. Just keep feeding it positive information. The classic song by Perry Como, "Accentuate the Positive," offers great words to live by:

"You gotta accentuate the positive,
Eliminate the negative,
An' latch on
To the affirmative,
Don't mess with Mister in-between!"

Chapter 1 assignment: *Start with a winning attitude.*
(Check off and record the date when you accomplish each activity).

1. □ / date _____ Go to your public library or a local well-stocked bookstore with a notepad and pen. Review periodicals such as *Entrepreneur Magazine, Home Business Magazine,* and others like them. Then take time to read key articles that capture your interest. Make notes.

2. □ / date _____ Seek out motivational books like *The Power of Intention, The Millionaire Mind, Think & Grow Rich,* and others like them. Review the chapter headings and make notes.

3. □ / date _____ Invest in yourself and your business by purchasing (or at least checking out of the library) one or more magazines and books in this topic area.

4. □ / date _____ Pray/meditate about your new venture.

5. □ / date _____ Write down five positive statements (commonly called "affirmations") about your business goal. Write them down as if you have already achieved them and review them twice a day. Examples are:

    •   I am a successful (*fill in the blank*) computer training consultant, Web site designer, resumé writer, bookkeeper, etc.

    •   I am making (*fill in the blank*) $1,000 a month, $3,000 a month, $5,000 a month, etc.

    •   I am happy and organized.

    •   I love serving and helping others achieve their dreams.

    •   I find time to build my business.

‹‹NOTES››

CHAPTER 2

Choose What You Enjoy

"Pleasure in the job puts perfection in the work."
Aristotle

Did you know you can make good money using your very own skills and talents? You don't have to do anything that doesn't interest you—you can actually make money doing something you enjoy! This doesn't mean that operating a business is an easy road to riches. It takes dedication, perseverance, organization, and a will to succeed. Whether you want to develop a business that will generate a full-time income or just supplement your current salary, the beauty of running your own business is that you set the hours. Decide what you want to do and then pursue it. Focus on something you already love doing because you won't tire of it easily.

Note: The time you have spent at a regular job is never wasted and actually is an advantage. You can use the skills you have acquired in the workplace to enhance your business. Take your increased level of expertise and sharpened abilities to the next level—to build and run your very own venture!

Evaluate your hobbies, interests, and talents

What is a talent—and how do you discover yours? Some people think they don't have any talents, but that isn't true. Everyone does. However, it's just that some talents aren't as easily recognized as others. Did you know that your talent lies in the area of your intense interest? It may reflect in a hobby or skill that you love to do, and would do even if no one paid you because it is so enjoyable and fulfilling.

Do you love

- designing?
- cooking?
- fixing gadgets and small appliances?
- drawing?
- gardening?

You may be surprised at the numbers of talents you have. You just need to figure out what you love to do and then turn that interest into $$$.

Your business can be a blend of your talents, experience, and hobbies. Take into consideration your work experience and the skills you have developed on the job (i.e., accounting, management, marketing, customer service, etc). Have you ever volunteered in a given field and found it fascinating? What is your educational background? What hobbies and recreation do you enjoy doing during your free time?

Write down your three favorite hobbies, skills or talents.

1.

2.

3.

Now think about how you might be able to incorporate the above into the following types of businesses.

Service businesses

Service types of businesses are always in demand, whether the economy is up or down. Look in the "Business Directory" section of your local newspaper for ideas. Examples of service businesses include: painters, housecleaners, wallpaper hangers, pet-sitters, typing, sewing/alterations, trash-haulers, and yard-workers, just to name a few. If you are orderly and systematic, perhaps you would like to help others organize and clean their yards/homes. Many service businesses lend themselves well to family enterprises; meaning that you can enlist most (if not all) family members to help with them, depending on their ages and the level of responsibility required.

Hauling business

In most cases, service businesses are easier and less expensive to start than other types of endeavors, especially if you already own necessary basic equipment. For instance, if you wanted to start a trash-hauling business (not to be confused with garbage collectors), you need a dependable good-sized pickup and tarp. You can help people in your neighborhood and community clean up their properties for a fee of (for example) $40 per load. Take it to the city dump and make $40-$80 (or more) for a few hours on a Saturday. Not bad money for a small investment of your time! When pricing your service, factor in the cost of gas and any other expenses. Some cities charge for dumping, so check for any costs involved with your local sanitation department, in advance.

Clothing alterations business

Do you like to sew and are you competent with a needle and thread? Why not consider an alterations business? It isn't as time-consuming as dressmaking and yields more money for the time spent on it. Your customers would be people who would rather repair or modify their clothing than purchase new outfits. Check with a few dry-cleaning establishments to see if they do alterations. Find out what they charge to get an idea of the going rate in your area. How long would it take you to pin up, press, and blind hem a skirt on your machine? Say you charge $10 to do it, and it took a total of 30 minutes time. That translates to $20 an hour if you hemmed two skirts or dresses. With enough clients, you could easily make $80.00 each day, $400 a week, and $1,200 a month for a four-hour daily investment of your time. And just think…you could make additional money replacing broken zippers and doing other miscellaneous alterations.

Typing business

Are you a fast and accurate typist? Do you have good spelling and punctuation skills? Do you own a computer and laser printer? You may consider operating a typing business out of your home. Check out the competition. Call around and see what others in your area charge for similar typing services. This kind of business lends itself well to repeat customers: do an excellent job at a reasonable price and you could build up a nice clientele and a steady stream of income!

Teach a class

Maybe you would rather make money teaching the skills you have acquired to others who would love to learn them. Check with your local library to see if you can book a room for an evening or a couple of hours on a Saturday for free or for a nominal charge. Some high schools will rent out rooms during the evening and (for an extra fee) equipment such as video projectors. Call your community education department (usually affiliated with your local school district) and see if they will put you on their roster as a teacher for the upcoming season.

Creative freelancing

Writers and graphic designers are in a specialty field, one that is a little harder to develop into a sustainable business. They are usually at the mercy of clients who need them for freelance work, and the work is often sporadic. However, success is much more possible when a writer and designer collaborate and combine their talents, then approach prospective clients.

Many "creatives" find the classified ad Web site www.craigslist.com a great place to find potential clients, advertise their services and also link up with potential business partners. You can craft an ad as long as you wish and post it within minutes of submission. Whereas the same ad in a traditional newspaper could cost $100 or more, ads on craigslist are free of charge. Favorite sections for creatives include *jobs*, *services* and *gigs*.

Consulting (personal coaching)

Perhaps you wish to strike out on your own, but want to stay in your chosen field. Many professionals go into consulting, and use their wisdom and experience to make money in their area of expertise. Establish an office area in your home and advertise to niche prospects. You can set your own hours, and work "by appointment only."

"Personal coaching" is a growing field—and may be your ticket to fulfillment and steady income. You can gain initial exposure by networking through the community and selected businesses, offering to speak for free to club members and employees on a relevant topic of interest.

Identify a need and then meet it

A business idea often emerges from a market need. Astute entrepreneurs then develop a product or service to meet that need. As an example, there was a woman who had struggled for many years to lose weight, but to no avail. One day, she came across some information about diet and nutrition that made sense to her. She shared that information with six friends and invited them over to her house where they could get together and discuss the "ups and downs" of trying to lose weight. The next week, those six friends brought some others who were interested in comparing notes and talking about weight loss. They went on the special diet and started shedding pounds. Word got around and, within two months, 40 people were congregating at the woman's home on a weekly basis. She ran out of room and moved the meetings to a building in town. She expected 50 or so people to show up at the new location and when 400 people showed up, a business was born. The lady was Jean Nidetch and she called her new company Weight Watchers.

Save your sanity with an appointment-based business

If possible, select a business you can run "by appointment only." This way you have control of your time. It will take some juggling at first, but you will preserve your sanity by setting your business hours around your personal life (for instance, in the evenings and on Saturdays). The following story illustrates one example of an "appointment only" type of business.

Linda was a single mom, raising two small children by herself. She worked during the day as a copywriter for a marketing company, but needed extra income to make ends meet and didn't want to work two jobs. During her college days, she had taken a class on job-searching skills and the part about resumé writing had really sparked her interest. She owned a computer and laser printer and decided to start a resumé business on the side.

Because she wanted to catch the eye of job seekers, Linda advertised in the "help wanted" section of the local newspaper with the slogan "Get a better job with a better resumé!" She personally did not think that general resumés were very effective, so she found a niche with job-targeted resumés. When possible, Linda would have her clients provide to her a description of their desired job. She would then interview them and pull into the resumé information from their background and experience that matched qualities the prospective employers were seeking.

Linda first interviewed the clients (either in person or over the phone) and she typed up the initial resumé. By appointment, they came to her home to review the resumé and at that time she would make any changes, and give them a master copy of the resumé (plus four copies on resumé paper) in a manila folder. At that time, the customer would pay her and she would give them a receipt. This sideline business fit nicely into her schedule because she could arrange the appointments at her convenience—around her family and full-time job. Linda developed a home-based business that matched her skills, talents, and interests with that of a market need.

Learn new skills

Perhaps there is something specific you would like to do—desktop publishing, for example—but you need more training. Invest in yourself and take some night classes. Many community education programs offer courses in the evenings at local high schools and other facilities. Booklets describing the various topics are usually printed on a seasonal basis. The library is a great resource of information about these classes, which are typically less expensive and shorter in duration than regular college classes.

- Write down the type of business you would like to create, (i.e., service business, teaching, consulting, creative, selling craft items on consignment, etc).

_____

_____

_____

- Write down one of your hobbies, skills or talents listed earlier.

_____

_____

_____

Now, brainstorm about ways you can combine your ideal business with one of your hobbies or skills. Write down your ideas now on a notepad or on the "notes" page at the end of this chapter.

Internet businesses

Web-based ventures usually require a higher front-end investment of time and money, but the income potential is unlimited. Other advantages: they are "open" 24/7, and don't require you to physically be at a certain location to run the business. To learn details about setting up an online business, visit a Web site such as www.oncallgeeks.com. It offers a free "10-Step Tutorial for Starting an Internet Business." You can also find books and magazines on the subject at your local library or bookstore.

Look before you leap

Some entrepreneurs would rather align their efforts with an established firm, such as a network marketing or direct sales company. It is wise to research an existing business opportunity thoroughly before investing time and money in it. How do you tell a legitimate one from a scam? Find out how long the firm has been in business, and if they are legally registered in their based state of operation. Consult the Better Business Bureau (BBB) for any complaints. If they haven't bothered to register their business name with the state, and if the BBB has registered any disputes or unresolved matters, steer clear of them. Visit www.bbb.org for more information.

No matter what you choose to do, it will take hard work and perseverance. However, doing something you can put your heart into will make it worth it…and much more enjoyable!

Chapter 2 assignment: *Choose what you enjoy.*
(Check off and record the date when you accomplish each activity).

1. □ / date _____ Ask someone close to you (a friend or relative) for an objective opinion of where they feel your talents and strengths lie.

2. □ / date _____ Explore ideas at your local bookstore or library by reviewing magazines and books directed to home businesses and entrepreneurs. You will find fascinating success stories of other business-builders and who knows…these stories may spark a fire of interest in areas you had not previously considered!

3. □ / date _____ Review your three favorite hobbies, skills or talents.

_____

_____

_____

_____

4. □ / date _____ Write down the one from #3 you think you could develop into a business.

_____

5. □ / date _____ List a way you could meet a market need with this skill (i.e., teach a class, fix something, provide a service, etc.).

_____

_____

_____

_____

‹‹NOTES››

Conduct Your Market Research

"A goal without a plan is just a wish."
Antoine de Saint-Exupery

Researching your target market is a very important part of starting a new business. This is where you do your homework and size up your potential customers. A target market is simply the unique group of potential customers you wish to influence. Identify a general target market and, whenever possible, serve a niche within that market—people whose special needs you will meet with your product or service. (Job seekers comprised the general target market for Linda's resumé service. If she were near a college town, her "niche" target market could also include recently graduated college students).

It's very important that you match your product or service to market needs. You may enjoy drawing cartoons, but you won't be able to build much of a business if no one is interested in purchasing them. You need customers and sales!

Research your target market

Studying your target market reveals information you need to create an advertising and marketing message. To begin, make a list of a typical person who is likely to purchase your products or services. It's easier if you think of your potential market as a person instead of a group, for evaluation purposes.

- Define your target market by giving your hypothetical person a name. _____

_____.

Now fill in the following blanks.

1) Age _____

2) Gender _____

3) Income level _____

3) Education level _____

4) Occupation _____

5) Types of stores shopped _____

6) Hobbies/recreational activities _____

- List this potential customer's needs and how you can meet them with your product or service.

_____

_____

_____

_____

_____

Consider developing a survey questionnaire about your product or service and distributing it to friends and acquaintances that you think may fit into your target market. This is a good way to evaluate interest in your product or service, to see if it is priced in the range that your market is willing to pay, and it is a way to let people know about your business in advance. You might consider giving your respondents a rain-check discount on your product or service for taking the time to fill out your survey questionnaire.

Following is a sample questionnaire for a potential resumé service:

Survey

1. If you were out of work or considering upgrading to a better-paying job, would you consider using a resumé service?
    Y___   N___

2. If the company's hours were flexible and you could meet with the resumé professional either in the day or evening by appointment, would that make a difference over choosing another company's service? Y___   N___

3. What is the highest price you would be willing to pay for a custom-written resumé that targeted the type of job you were looking for? A. $65 B. $75 C. $85 D. $95

4. Would it make a difference to you whether the resumé service was conducted from a home or an office? Y___   N___

5. If you would be interested in such a service in the future, please write your name and contact information below. As a "thank you" for taking the time to fill out this survey, you are eligible to receive a 10 percent discount on a custom-written resumé from (insert your company name here).

_____

_____

_____

_____

_____

_____

Evaluate your competition

Healthy competition is at the heart of a free society. You could compare it to a game like football or even call it a "friendly war." You must know how your competition thinks and acts so you can develop your marketing strategy. If possible, target a smaller "niche" group, which is a subset of a larger group of customers. (We'll talk more about niche marketing a little later). Your competition is any company engaged in marketing the same type or similar products/services to yours. It could be a sole proprietor, a large corporation, or something in-between.

Researching your competition will help you create a strategy for attracting potential customers. You can gather information on your competitors by visiting their place of business, calling them on the phone, or by visiting their Web site.

Check around and research what people are doing with similar products or services. Find out how much they charge and where their customers come from. How are their businesses doing? Do they advertise in the local telephone directory? Word of mouth? Radio spots? The more you know about your competitors, the more you can differentiate your business from theirs, in a good way. Learn from them and perhaps you can even serve a subset of their general customer base. By studying your competitors' strengths and weaknesses, you can tell what works and what doesn't. In the long run, you will save yourself a lot of time, money, and headaches.

Make sure your quality is high, your price is fair, and your service is excellent. Then you will never have to worry about what others are or aren't doing. You will build a base of loyal customers who will, in turn, refer their friends to you.

Establish your competitive advantages

What makes your product or service different from that of the competition? Can you beat their price, quality, reliability and/or customer satisfaction? If your office is located in your home, you also have the personal advantage of lower overhead (not paying extra rent and utilities). You then have the option of passing along the savings in the form of lower prices.

Besides competing head-to-head with a competitor and vying for the same customer segment, there are other options to consider when trying to corner a particular market share:

1) **Establish a new type of market category**. This takes a lot of courage and risk but could yield unlimited potential income. (What would America be like today if some enterprising person had not thought up the concept of a health food store?).

2) **Be the first in your area to offer a particular kind of product or service**. Then—through creative advertising and marketing—generate a demand for it!

3) **Improve upon an existing product or service** (by reducing its cost or perhaps by adding to its features).

The advantages of niche or "specialty" marketing

First, you need to identify the general customer base to which you would like to sell your product or service. Once you identify this market, you should focus on a subset or "niche" of that group. A niche market can be defined as "a group of customers who have the same specialized interests and needs." They also must want/need what you have to offer. With niche marketing, you can hone your sales message to the specifically defined interests of people in that set.

For instance, say you design Web sites. Instead of offering Web-page design services to just anyone, you could develop Web sites for a specialty group—realtors, for example.

Serving a small niche market can give you a competitive advantage because other businesses may overlook the opportunity.

If you tailor your sales message to the specific needs and interests of your niche market, you'll enjoy a sharp increase in your sales and profits.

- Define your target customer market.
1) Write a description of your general customer base.

_____

_____

_____

2) Write a description of a subset or "niche" of that market.

_____

_____

_____

It would be helpful to start developing a file of niche marketing campaigns. You're exposed to them all the time, especially through so-called "junk mail." Start saving these direct response ads and note the ones that appeal to you and why. Likewise, keep examples of those that "turn you off" and the reasons. Then you will create a foundation on which to pattern your own marketing strategies.

Conducting market research in the beginning stages of your business will save you a lot of wasted time later on. You will know your customers and be able to develop subsequent advertising and marketing strategies to capture their attention and their business. Always be alert to new ideas you can incorporate into your own venture by keeping a sharp eye out for advertising and marketing concepts that attract you. This will help you to formulate your own strategies and increase your awareness of what attracts customers and also what doesn't really do the job.

Chapter 3 assignment: *Conduct your market research.*
(Check off and record the date when you accomplish each activity).

1. ☐ / date _____ Develop a survey questionnaire about your product or service and distribute it to friends and acquaintances that you think may fit into your target market.

2. ☐ / date _____ Identify direct competitors in your local area.

3. ☐ / date _____ What are their market niches (low prices and quality goods)?

4. ☐ / date _____ Examine their marketing tactics. (Soft sell? Aggressive hard-sell?) Or gimmicky like the Southern California car dealer who brought out exotic animals at different times on his television commercials and introduced each as his dog Spot? This was a very unusual attention-grabber. Unusual—but effective!

5. ☐ / date _____ Study favorite tactics you feel have worked best with customers and make note of advertising ploys you do not like.

6. ☐ / date _____ Start a file of niche marketing techniques and examples you would like to emulate, as well as those you would like to avoid.

7. ☐ / date _____ Identify your market niche—that small, unique segment of consumers who need a specific product or service.

8. ☐ / date _____ Identify key areas that will set you apart from the competition and use these as marketing points in your advertising.

‹‹NOTES››

CHAPTER 4

Your Business Structure and Identity

"Drive thy business or it will drive thee."
Benjamin Franklin

Selecting your business structure is like framing a house. It determines the size, shape, and solidarity of your enterprise. Following is a list of the common types of business organizations. Examine them carefully, then decide which one is best for you.

Sole Proprietorship: Easy and inexpensive to start, a sole proprietorship is the most common type of business structure and the easiest to dissolve. In this type of arrangement, one individual or married couple in business makes all the decisions and enjoys all the benefits. However, as sole proprietor, you and your business are viewed as one and the same: your personal assets are not separate from your business assets. This means you are personally responsible for any claims against your business (i.e. lawsuits or tax liens).

General Partnership: A General Partnership is composed of two or more persons (usually not a married couple) who agree to contribute money, labor, and/or skill to a business. In a partnership, the parties enrich the business with their complementary skills and share the financial burden. Before you embark upon a partnership, it's wise to discuss and identify job responsibilities and ownership percentages, as well as rules for dissolving the partnership. Formal terms of the partnership are usually defined in a written partnership agreement.

Limited Partnership: A Limited Partnership is comprised of one or more general partners and one or more limited partners. The general partners handle the business and share responsibility for profits and losses. Limited partners share in the profits of the business, but their losses are limited to the extent of their investment. Limited partners usually do not manage daily operations of the business.

Limited Liability Partnership (LLP): This type of arrangement is similar to a General Partnership except that, in most cases, one partner does not have personal liability for the negligence of another. Accountants and lawyers most often use the LLP arrangement.

Corporation: There are "pros" and "cons" to starting a "C" or regular corporation. The good news is that your personal assets are not vulnerable to lawsuits or tax liens. The bad news is that it's more expensive to ramp up and maintain a corporation from the standpoint of business fees, legal filings, annual costs, and taxes. And with a corporation, you are taxed twice: first, on profits earned at the corporate level and second, on those resulting from individual profit sharing. Corporations may be formed for profit or nonprofit purposes.

Subchapter "S" Type Corporation: Enjoy the perks of incorporating without the double taxation of a "C" corporation by organizing a Subchapter or "S" Corporation. In this type of set-up, corporate profits are channeled directly to the business owners in the form of personal income. Another advantage is that corporate losses are subtracted from other personal income.

Limited Liability Company (LLC): An LLC is a hybrid of a partnership and a corporation, and must have at least two owners. With an LLC, you get the tax benefits of a partnership and the personal asset protection of a corporation. Check to see if LLCs are recognized as legitimate business set-ups in your state (not all states allow them). A Limited Liability Company can operate any legal for-profit business or activity, except for banking or insurance.

- Write down the type of business organization you think will best meet your needs.

Your professional identity

Your business will be hallmarked by your business or "corporate" identity—a combination of your business name, your "tagline" or slogan, and the logo you select. (You don't have to be a "corporation" to have a corporate identity). Be sure your corporate identity is clearly defined and easy to remember, as it can either attract or drive away potential customers. If you haven't yet developed your corporate identity, brainstorm with others for ideas. Following are some guidelines that will help you.

Your business name

The name you select for your business should reflect the type of product or service you offer. It shouldn't be too long and should be easy to pronounce. (This means no guessing as to how to say it). The name should also be easy to remember and indicate the nature of your firm. For instance, "Mark Johnson Enterprises" doesn't tell the type of business it is, but "Mark's Landscaping Service" does.

- Brainstorm and write down four possible business names that would reflect your business function.

1.

2.

3.

4.

Research your business name

Make sure your business name is available and unregistered. You don't want to go to all the time and expense of developing your corporate identity, only to discover your name is already taken. Go online to research previously registered trade names and trademarks on a state and federal level.

Once you've made sure another company isn't using the name, protect your unique name and logo with a trademark. To research names, apply for a trademark, and associated activities, contact the United States Patent and Trademark Office at Crystal Plaza 3, Room 2C02, Washington, D.C., 20231, call 1-800-786-9199, or go online at www.uspto.gov.

Apply for a "DBA" in your state

Contact your city, county or state business licensing agency to register your fictitious or "assumed" business name for a DBA or "doing business as" license. The fee is usually nominal, in some states as low as $20 per year for a sole proprietorship. If applicable, check with your city's business licensing division to see if they require a home-based business permit. (Some cities do, and some don't). They may have restrictions regarding the number of customers that can visit your business establishment at a time because of parking restrictions, noise that will bother your neighbors, and similar regulations.

Develop a brief slogan or "tagline"

Describe your product, service, or business and its mission, ideally in five words or less, to keep it short and snappy. This will set you apart from others in the marketplace and give potential buyers an indication of what your business is about.

How many of these famous taglines do you remember and can you readily name the companies and products they represent? "You deserve a break today." "Don't leave home without it." "Reach out and touch someone." "The quicker picker-upper." "The breakfast of champions."

- Brainstorm and write down four possible taglines that support or tie into your business name.

1.

2.

3.

4.

Create your logo

A logo is a picture or symbol that visually identifies your business, product or service. A memorable logo positioned next to the tagline will further embed your corporate identity in your customers' minds. For example, everyone is familiar with the McDonald's Corporation "golden arches" logo.

Color, form, and font should work together to create an appealing logo. Select an icon or design that reflects an accurate image of your business to its target market. A professional graphic designer can help develop your logo.

- Brainstorm and describe four possible pictures or symbols that support, or tie into, your business name.

1.

2.

3.

4.

Your business structure and identity both create your unique fingerprint separating you from the rest of the companies around. Don't take these aspects of your endeavor lightly. Think through and consider all your options before giving them your final stamp of approval. Your fledgling company's reputation is at stake. Create for your business the best face you can give it!

Chapter 4 assignment: *Your business structure and identity.*
(Check off and record the date when you accomplish each activity).

1. □ / date ____ Decide what type of business structure you will work under (i.e., sole proprietorship, partnership, corporation, "S" corporation, or LLC).

2. □ / date ____ Select your business name. Remember, it should reflect the type of product or service you offer.

3. □ / date ____ Make sure your business name is available and unregistered.

4. □ / date ____ Develop a slogan or tagline that incorporates your company's mission statement.

5. □ / date ____ Create a memorable logo.

Selecting Your Office Location

*"Destiny is no matter of chance. It is a matter of choice.
It is not a thing to be waited for; it is a thing to be achieved."*
William Jennings Bryan

The next step is figuring out where you will locate your office. A home-based business doesn't necessarily mean you maintain your business at your residence. Each situation is different. You can work in a professional office setting, yet still have the flexibility of working your hours around your private or family life. Following are some pros and cons of maintaining a separate office or one inside your home:

Pros for an office separate from your home
- No background noise (family conversations; pets barking)
- A more professional image
- More privacy (clients can't show up unexpectedly at your front door)

Pros for an office in your home
- Convenience
- Saves money (gas, utilities, office rent, childcare fees)
- Saves time

Organizing your home office
Every home offers unique options for potential office space. When considering your home office needs, you should evaluate the following: (a) How will customers access your office, and will they need an outside entrance? (b) Do you have an area away from noise and distractions? (c) How much space will your office equipment require? (d) Will you

31

need space to accommodate other workers? Look around your home and be creative—you can find extra space almost anywhere. Some areas to consider are:

- *An extra bedroom*— **Advantages**: It affords privacy because it's away from the noise of other rooms. And, in most cases, the bedroom is already set up with telephone connections. **Disadvantage:** Visitors will probably have to walk through the rest of your home to get there.

- *Your own bedroom.* **Advantage:** Even in a small apartment, you can convert a corner of your bedroom to an office area by relocating the dresser, perhaps into the closet. **Disadvantage:** You may be sleeping in cramped quarters.

- *Living room, family room or dining room.* **Advantages**: Your customers won't have to walk through your home to reach your office. Also, you can use screens or other partitions, like bookcases, to create a semi-private workspace. **Disadvantage**: Friends and family usually congregate in these types of areas, so they aren't noise-proof.

- *Nooks (i.e., under the stairs or in a walk-in closet).* **Advantage**: You can use a small area of unused space to help turn a profit-building business. **Disadvantage**: You will need to be conservative about the sizes of office equipment you choose. *Tip*: Make space in a closet by removing the door and adding bookshelves along the upper wall. Use a small table as a desk for your computer equipment.

- *Garage.* You may consider using your garage as office space, if it is relatively clean and neat. **Advantages**: It can be fixed up as a "standalone" office because it is separate from your home. It also meets most building code requirements because it already has walls, a floor, electricity, and a roof. **Disadvantages**: You'll probably need to add air-conditioning, heating, and insulation for temperature control, and perhaps subflooring and carpeting. And, by law, a garage door cannot be used as a business entrance, so additional remodeling and a building permit might be required.

Your "office away from home"

Locating an office that suits your specific needs and budget will take time spent looking around and doing comparison shopping. Some considerations might include: How much square footage will you need? Are there computer and fax hookups available? Will you have to sign a rental lease agreement for a specified amount of time? Are utility payments included in the cost or do you have to pay them in addition to the monthly lease amount? Is the office furnished or do you have to supply your own desk, table, chairs, etc? Is there adequate parking for your clients? Is it in a desirable and accessible area of town? Sometimes you can share office space in a "co-op" type of arrangement and cut some costs that way.

Take your time and make sure you find an office that you like. Also, try to look at it from your potential client's point of view, and make sure it will give them a favorable impression of you and your business.

Basic equipment

It's a good idea to start your business with as many helpful tools as possible. This list gives you a general idea and you can adapt your own list, according to your needs:

- Computer and printer
- Fax
- Cell phone
- Copy machine
- Internet access

A reminder—for those times you feel overwhelmed

Conducting the left-brained aspects of business building isn't very exciting. At times, you may wonder why you should go to all the trouble of starting a business, especially when so many fail their in their first or second year. First of all, if you go into business armed with knowledge, preparation, persistence, and a positive attitude, chances are very strong your enterprise will succeed. Second, the reasons you **should** go into business for yourself (especially based from home) greatly outweigh the reasons why you shouldn't. The following are just a few examples:

- **Financial freedom**. Self-employment gives you an additional source of income.

- **Make as much money as you'd like**. You can give yourself a raise simply by increasing your efforts!

- **Greater flexibility of time**. You don't have to work your personal/family life around a second or third job. Instead, you schedule the work around your life.

- **Pay less to the IRS**. Self-employment offers many tax advantages, but you must keep careful records.

- **Increases confidence in your abilities**. Creating a business "from the ground up" gives you a sense of fulfillment and accomplishment.

- **Provides security in these shaky economic times**. If, for any reason, you should lose your primary source of income, you need not panic if your business is already established. You have another immediate avenue for your livelihood. Having previously done the groundwork (the hardest part), you can focus your efforts fulltime and enjoy a corresponding increase in revenue.

Chapter 5 assignment: *Selecting your office space.*
(Check off and record the date when you accomplish each activity).

1. □ / date _____ Describe where your ideal office will be held (at home or away from home).

   _____

   _____

   _____

2. □ / date _____ Describe how you will furnish your office.

   _____

   _____

   _____

3. □ / date _____ Look at your office from your potential client's point of view and make note of ideas for improvement.

   _____

   _____

   _____

   _____

4. □ / date _____ Make a list of basic equipment you will need.

   _____

   _____

   _____

   _____

5. □ / date _____ From this chapter, list your three favorite reasons for becoming self-employed (i.e., financial freedom, greater flexibility of time, security, etc.).

_____

_____

_____

_____

_____

Advertising and Marketing

*"He who has a thing to sell
and goes and whispers in a well,
is not so apt to get the dollars
as he who climbs a tree and hollers!"*
Unknown

O ne of the best things about being your own boss is you get to direct all of your efforts the way you want. No one is there telling you what to do. Of course, this puts a great responsibility on your shoulders, requiring lots of hard work and a strong sense of self-discipline, but provides a definite growing experience. What an exciting adventure!

One thing's for sure—you can't be shy when it comes to promoting your products or services. You have to shout about it! However, you can't broadcast to just anyone. As emphasized earlier, you must study your potential customers and know their likes, dislikes, and buying habits. If you know your customers, you can design a compelling message—especially directed to their needs, wants, and desires.

Publicize your new enterprise

Get your business off to a robust start by spreading the word about how great it is and what you have to offer. In other words, *climb a tree and holler*! Build a solid reputation for service and quality. This will create credibility and confidence with your customers.

Prepare an advertising budget

It's a hard fact of the entrepreneurial life—you can't run a business without operating capital (the green stuff). You'll need to figure in advance how much you'll need to advertise and market your products or services, so you can cover all expenses. Make a list and corresponding costs of items such as business cards, stationery, promotional brochures, printing costs, and advertising fees. If you plan on enlisting the services of freelancers, such as a graphic designer or copywriter, you will need to incorporate these costs into your budget. Keep a record of each expense as you pay it, and maintain control of your advertising budget. If you need additional money, raise it in creative ways as suggested in Chapter 7.

> *Tip*: When starting out, you'll want to stretch your marketing budget as far as you can with the least expensive forms of advertising—such as distributing business cards or flyers to people in your area of business. Once you start making a predictable income from your business, you can expand into more sophisticated advertising avenues.

Pricing your products or services

When determining the costs of your products or services, you should consider four important factors:

- Overhead cost of developing and bringing your product or service to market.

- Perceived value of your product or service. (The more your product or service is valued by your customers, the more you will be able to charge for it).

- How much the competition charges for similar offerings.

- Your desired profit.

Determine your end price by:

1) Figuring out a rough estimate of your overhead _____
_____.

2) Figuring out your desired profit _____
_____.

3) Factoring in the above costs, write down the end price of your product/service_____
_____.

For more precise calculations, see the section "Establishing fees" in Chapter 7.

Sales strategy

Next, decide how you will advertise and then distribute your product or service. One facet of business success is built upon addressing customer concerns, meeting all deadlines, and delivering your products or services in a timely, courteous, and professional manner. Everyone loves a bargain, so think of ways you can offer a discount or incentive. For example, advertise a grand opening special at 20 percent off the regular price of your product or service. Or how about bundling a free service with your primary one (i.e., free cover letter with every resumé order by a certain date).

Develop your ad campaign

Your promotional and advertising literature represents your business to the public. Make sure your business cards, brochures, etc. make a great impression by having them professionally written and designed. A consistent look to your marketing materials will also enhance your company image.

For the most effective advertising approach, determine how you can reach the largest number of your target customers. There are several advertising options, and you should carefully evaluate each of them to see which will best meet your marketing goals. They are categorized according to their relative costs.

Most expensive

Television and radio
Television and radio are excellent for targeting large numbers of people. However, air time is expensive and because the ads are brief, you'll need to advertise frequently, and on a regular basis, to get your message across.

Internet
The World Wide Web offers an opportunity for entrepreneurs to create a Web site where 1) customers can learn about your product or service, and 2) if your site is e-commerce enabled, they can easily purchase from you online. Other advertising options on the Internet include affiliate programs, banner ads on other Web sites, and e-mail marketing.

Direct mail
Direct mail involves sending potential customers brochures, letters, or postcards by mail from pre-qualified mailing lists. The purpose is to interest prospects in requesting more information about your products or services. Personalize each direct mail piece by using the prospect's name, if possible. Make it easy to read and understand and be sure your contact information is prominently displayed, so they can obtain follow-up information or make a purchase. Follow your direct mailings with phone calls or e-mails to your potential customers.

Tip: For examples of direct mail pieces, look in your mailbox. You receive direct mail every week. Although sometimes regarded as "junk mail," you can use these as examples of what to do and what not to do. Start collecting and evaluating them for their impact. File the ones you like the best and use them as examples for future mailing ideas. The most targeted (and probably most effective) type of direct mail will be addressed to you personally, not to "current resident."

Press (media) kit

The press kit is a folder of information designed to publicize and give a favorable impression of your company. It also saves time for busy reporters who wish to craft an accurate story (whether via newspaper articles, television, radio or other medium). Contents of the kit may include professional profiles of key company executives or officers, black and white or color photos, a fact sheet about your organization, a business card, recent press releases, company literature, and copies of published articles. Send your press kit when an editor, publisher, or producer seeks information about your company.

Moderately expensive

Classified ads

Many fledgling businesses have successfully used the classified ad sections of newspapers for widespread publicity. And don't forget the advantage of 21st century technology. Online classified ads (like craigslist) reach the broadest consumer base of all. First, consider placing a classified "test ad" to gauge consumer response and run it for several weeks. Jay Conrad Levinson, author of *Guerrilla Marketing*, gives these valuable tips about classified advertising:

- "If you are a good writer, write your own classified-ad copy. If not, go to a pro.

- Don't rely on the person who takes the ads to write your copy.

- Word your ad in such a way that it contrasts with other ads in the same section. And choose that section…very carefully.

- Advertise in the proper category. Make that plural. You may want to place your ad in more than one category.

- Classified ads often outdraw display ads. So don't think that just because an ad has no picture and doesn't cost much, it's not going to be effective."

Brochures

Your brochure is your "sales" piece, where you pitch your product or service. Focus on benefits, in which you describe what you can do for your potential customer. Testimonials from satisfied clients can powerfully communicate your message. The brochure should be easy to read (without fancy language and big words). It should be designed with appealing headlines, attractive graphics (and photos, if appropriate). Brochures can be created and folded in various types of panels such as z-fold, gatefold, single-fold, etc. Ask a professional graphic designer or print house representative for examples.

Stationery

Personalized stationery made of high quality paper gives your business an upscale image. Print all of your contact information on it (phone and fax numbers, mailing, Web site, and e-mail addresses) and company name and logo. Use this stationery for all business correspondence. It's a worthwhile investment.

Business cards

Business cards are inexpensive to produce, yet essential to growing your enterprise. They should include your contact information, and be attractive and easy to read. Complete your business card with an appealing logo and a short, catchy mission statement.

Least expensive

Flyers

Of all the advertising mediums, flyers are considered the least expensive to produce. Another plus: you can pack a lot of marketing information into a full-page flyer! (Don't forget to include your contact info). Post your flyers on store bulletin boards, on car windshields, and on doorknobs in your neighborhood. However, be sure and get permission before distributing them.

Press releases and articles

Press releases and articles offer two exciting avenues for free publicity. Through them, you can reach a wide range of people without spending a single advertising dollar. Ideally, your press release should be only one page long—concise, yet dynamic. Like a resumé, your press release should "sing your praises." Send it to the editor of the publication and follow up your submission with a phone call a day or two later. Be polite, yet enthusiastic, when you make your contact!

Newsletters

Newsletter articles also increase exposure of your company and are great to include in your press kit. Look in the directory of trade newsletters under your subject area (check your local university library, in their reference book section). Contact the newsletter editors and offer to send them a press kit. Once you've been featured in lesser-known publications, you can use the exposure as a steppingstone to get published in those with larger circulations. Also consider contacting online e-zines, as well. Just type in a word that explains your subject into your favorite search engine and see how many potential sites pop up!

Public speaking engagements

Contact local civic clubs and directors of educational programs. Offer to give free speeches in your area of expertise. Tap into the radio talk show market, as well. They are always keeping an eye (and ear) out for new speakers. Once you are featured on talk radio shows you will be viewed as an expert in your field, and more avenues of publicity will open to you.

Magazine and newspaper articles

First, outline several general article ideas with an angle relevant to the newspaper or magazine you are targeting. Then write a query letter (also known as a "publicity pitch"). Editors appreciate reviewing ideas instead of full-fledged articles. When articles instead of query letters are sent without prior communication with the magazine, they are considered "unsolicited manuscripts." If the ideas you pitch pique their interest, they will ask for the entire article, which is then considered a "solicited manuscript." Instead of receiving payment for the piece, ask if you can advertise your home business at the end. If you're unsure of how to write query letters and articles, enlist the help of a professional writer.

Networking

Network with other professionals to strengthen your marketing position. Your primary goal is to promote exposure and advertising of your business. For an annual fee, you can join your local Chamber of Commerce and establish valuable local business-to-business connections. Benefits of membership in your Chamber of Commerce include:

- Introducing you to new customers
- Referring potential customers in response to inquiries
- Giving your new business exposure in your local newspaper (business section)
- Providing business startup information
- Networking at weekly business luncheons
- Helping you locate proper facilities for meetings and conventions
- Keeping you informed about events affecting your business—from political issues to survey results

Bartering

Remember reading about the old-fashioned trading post or general store where settlers came to trade their harvests for basic commodities, such as flour and sugar? Well, this same idea is still alive and well in the 21st century. You can save considerable advertising budget money by swapping goods and services. Jay Conrad Levinson says:

> "Guerrillas learn of the exciting world of barter by ... closely examining *BarterNews*...At least 500 magazines will trade ad space for whatever it is they need.

> "Policies vary at publications, however, and trades must be individually negotiated. Remember that everyone needs something. By learning what your selected media need, you may be able to set up a money-saving trade... To give you an inkling of the magnitude of barter in today's economy, consider that in 1996 more than 55 percent of media was not purchased but obtained by barter."

Partner with others

Team up with someone who has complementary skills and abilities and you'll build your business twice as fast as you would by going solo. Partner with one or more people who are willing to work just as hard as you, and who share the same vision. Don't worry about the profits. There will be plenty to go around with more people sharing the workload. Working with others also spurs your motivation. It's easy to get discouraged when you are the only one taking the risks and when you're the only driving force. However, if others are counting on you, then it gives you more incentive to hunker down and get the job done.

Collaborate with people who have talents and strong points in areas other than your own. For instance, if you are a "right-brained creative" (writer or artist), you may wish to team up with a pragmatic "left-brained business manager" who can go out and beat the pavement, get clients for you, and negotiate deals. Napoleon Hill calls this type of arrangement the "Master Mind." He explains it as "coordination of knowledge and effort, in a spirit of harmony, between two or more people, for the attainment of a definite purpose."

Ethics

Make sure you team up with people who are honest. Sometimes it's hard to tell, and you have to go by intuition. You don't want to link up with people who will cheat you *or* your customers. Customers are the lifeblood of a successful business and nothing will drive them away faster than a company they perceive is unethical. Besides that, it's just a good practice to let honesty guide your actions. The maxim "Honesty is the best policy" will never go out of style.

- Brainstorm and take a moment to write down the names of at least six people with whom you think you would like to partner in a business. Especially select names of those whose skills and talents would complement yours. (For instance, if you are more creative than good at recordkeeping, select someone who has strong accounting skills). List the names in preference, with the strongest first.

1.

2.

3.

4.

5.

6.

Contact these people about your business idea without asking them to join at first, to see how they respond to it.

Evaluate your marketing strategies

Measure the value of your marketing strategies by discovering where most of your customer leads originate. Count how many customers come from each marketing effort (i.e., flyers, radio, word-of-mouth, etc.). How do you find out this information? Provide surveys to new customers or simply ask them where they heard about your company. Next, evaluate the quality of these leads by tracking the number that actually generated sales. This will give you a general idea of which approaches attract the most qualified customers.

Time it right

When developing your marketing campaign, a key strategy is timing. Try to create a promotional angle around something distinctive about your business, a connection between what you have to offer and a current news topic or trend or an upcoming event. These and additional ideas are found in the book *6 Steps to Free Publicity* by Marcia Yudkin.

Communicating with your customer

Make it easy for prospective customers to contact you. How will you handle business correspondence, phone or e-mail inquiries? Will you use your home address as your business address? All of these are important considerations.

- List at least three ways you would like customers to communicate with you.

1.

2.

3.

The Web

A Web presence will give your business greater credibility. However, it's expensive and time-consuming to develop an entire Web site. Why not consider a single Web page, for now? Many Internet Service Providers (ISPs) give you free Web page space, as part of their package. To start, ask a Web-savvy graphic designer to create one page where you can put a basic description of your business, some eye-catching graphics, your address and phone number. To prevent spam you might want to offer an online form where someone can submit an e-mail to you, rather than posting your e-mail address. This simple Web page is all you need, at the beginning. Later on, you can expand your site into greater depth.

Tips for review

Read this chapter carefully, several times if necessary. Your business success greatly depends on how, when, and where you advertise. Keep track of your advertising expenses and select the avenue that will give you the most "bang for your buck." Most of all, keep your lines of communication open!

Chapter 6 assignment: *Advertising and marketing.*

(Check off and record the date when you accomplish each activity).

1. □ / date _____ Prepare an advertising budget. Make a list and corresponding costs of items such as business cards, stationery, promotional brochures, printing, and advertising fees.

2. □ / date _____ Figure out pricing for your products or services.

3. □ / date _____ Develop your advertising campaign by creating your promotional literature.

4. □ / date _____ Determine how you will reach the largest segment of your target customers.

5. □ / date _____ Set dates to accomplish each advertising strategy (i.e., classified ads, flyers, radio ads, etc.) and mark them on your calendar.

Tax Deductions and Other Important Money Matters

"Money frees you from doing things you dislike.
Since I dislike doing nearly everything, money is handy."
Groucho Marx

O rganizing the basics might not be as exciting as advertising and marketing, but is nevertheless crucial to your long-term accomplishment. All serious businesspeople dedicated to creating solid enterprises make time for the "nuts and bolts" of commerce, like keeping proper records. Every time you transact anything to do with your business, record it on your receipt and file it in a designated place, like a manila envelope. When tax time comes, you'll breathe easily and won't have to hunt all over and backtrack, trying to reconstruct your deductions.

Following are examples of common business deductions. (Consult with a qualified accountant for specific details concerning your individual tax situation).

Auto—Keep track of all your business-related auto expenditures or just subtract the current allowable "cents per mile" for each business mile driven.

Going into business—Costs of starting a business are capital expenses, which must be deducted over the first five years you are in business. Once you're in business, you can deduct expenses such as advertising, utilities, office supplies and repairs.

Education—Fees for seminars and classes can be deducted as business expenses if they are related to your current enterprise.

Business entertaining—If you pay the tab for entertaining present or prospective customers, you may deduct 50 percent of the cost if it is directly related to the business and business is discussed, or is associated with the business (i.e., the entertainment takes place immediately before or after a business discussion). Be sure to record the purpose and transaction on your receipt so you can validate your business-related connection.

Travel—Business travel expense deductions include cost of plane fare, operating your car, taxis, lodging, meals, shipping business materials, dry-cleaning, telephone calls, faxes, and tips.

Interest—If you use credit or take out a personal loan to finance business purchases, the interest and carrying charges are fully tax deductible. It's especially important to keep accurate records proving the money was put into your business, and not used for something else.

Advertising and promotion—Costs associated with advertising your products or services (i.e., business cards, newspaper/telephone directory ads, etc.) are tax deductible. Promotional costs that create "business goodwill" (like sponsoring a Little League team) are also deductible as long as there is a definite link between the sponsorship and your business.

Your family—Even though you personally don't qualify as an employee of your business, you may be able to create deductible medical coverage for your spouse, your children and yourself by hiring your spouse in your business. Your children can work for your business, beginning around age 8, until they have a "real" job and are on their own. Transferring income away from your business to your children helps lower your tax liability. They are usually in a lower tax bracket, or may not even owe taxes on the money paid to them.

Examples of additional "write-offs"

The following are just a few ideas of other business expense deductions.

- Purchase of audio and video tapes, DVDs and CDs related to improving business skills
- Office supplies
- Bank service charges
- Business association dues
- Business gifts
- Purchase of business-related magazines and books
- Consultant fees
- Online computer services related to business
- Parking and meters
- Postage
- Fees associated with business-related seminars and trade shows
- Taxi and bus fare
- Business-related telephone transactions/bills

Financing your venture

While your business is still in the planning stage, make a list of all your startup expenses. They may include (but are not limited to): inventory, licenses, permits, merchant account fees, office supplies, office equipment, and those associated with advertising and marketing. Then figure out how much you will have to bring in each month to survive. Most entrepreneurs have limited start-up funding resources available to them. It's best to leave credit cards alone unless you're sure of a quick return on your investment. Some novel ideas for raising seed money to bootstrap your enterprise include:

- Garage sales
- Selling extra furniture, appliances, and other household possessions
- Borrowing from your savings account or 401K
- Selling stocks
- Selling unwanted items online on auction sites like eBay
- Buying items for cheap at yard sales and reselling them via online auction sites, like eBay or online classified ads like craigslist.

The wisest course when beginning a business is to "start small" and expand from there. In other words, don't go into massive debt to finance your endeavor. However, if you do need funding from a lending institution, a business plan is essential.

Your business plan

Developing a business plan is an excellent way to keep on track and focused and it will come in handy, should you need additional financing from a bank or other lending institution. Creating a business plan takes time, research, and work but helps you evaluate and establish your goals. Following are some main elements and sections of a business plan:

1. Cover sheet
2. Statement of purpose
3. Table of contents
   - Description of the business
   - Marketing
   - Finances
   - Management

If you use a business plan to seek funding, your lender will also require an executive summary, supporting documents and financial projections as part of your application package. For further details on business plans and how they work, visit the United States Small Business Administration Web site at www.sba.gov.

Bookkeeping

It's absolutely imperative that you keep track of money coming in and going out of your business *each day*. Whether you use a manual-entry ledger or a software bookkeeping system like QuickBooks or Quicken, you must identify and log every transaction associated with your operation. You can purchase standard packages at any office supply store. If this part of the business intimidates you, ask someone who is good with accounting and math to help you set up a system that meets your business needs.

Sales tax identification number

If you're selling products, you will need to keep track of—and charge tax on—sales for state tax purposes. You will be asked to report transaction totals on a regular basis. Contact your state tax commission office for forms and details. (Look in your local phone directory or online for contact information).

Set up a business checking account

You can obtain a business checking account after you have filed your DBA and received your official license. The bank will require proof of business licensing before you can set up the account. A business checking account is especially helpful to separate your personal banking transactions from those associated with your commercial transactions for tax record purposes.

Credit cards and merchant accounts

It's hard to do business in today's modern world without accepting credit cards. However, be very careful before you sign on the dotted line to set up a merchant account. Many entrepreneurs have been burned by fast-talking card service vendors who linked them with a credit card machine leasing company, only to find out they were stuck with the agreement, whether they used the machines or not.

A woman who had been out of work for a year, and consequently ended up with a low credit rating, decided to start a business of her own to improve her circumstances. As soon as she filed her business name with the state, her mailbox was flooded with merchant account offers. She decided to look into a card service company that looked legitimate. When she called the company, a smooth-talking young man convinced her over the phone to apply for an account. He faxed her an application and within a day of the time she faxed it back he told her she was "approved." She told him she wasn't ready for an account yet; she hadn't officially organized her business and was just in the preliminary stages. However, before she knew it, she was talked into signing up for a merchant account and leasing credit card machines to a tune of more than $2,500.

Her payments ended up more than $60 per month to the credit card machine leasing company after all fees were added, and $35.00 per month to the "middleman" card service company for the life of the lease: a contract period of three years. Some things happened in her life that postponed her business setup and she tried to get out of the lease by sending the machines back to the company, but the leasing company said she would have to find someone to take over her lease. More than a year and a half later, she was still paying nearly $100 every month—with nothing to show for it but two credit card machines lying unused in her bedroom closet.

The moral of this story is: if someone tries to fast-talk you into signing up for a merchant account, tell them you need time to think about it. Evaluate your business status and once it is solid (*meaning you have customers ready to buy your product or service*) contact your bank or credit union to see if their terms would work for you.

Establishing fees

How do you know how much to charge? Find out what people operating similar businesses are charging and you'll have a basis upon which to determine your fees. Look in your local phone book to locate similar businesses. Then go down the list and call each one.

If you're a courageous pioneer and are breaking new ground, you should charge a combination of what you feel you need to make, what you think is fair, and what the market will bear. Determine what you feel you should make per year "net" (net income is what you make after subtracting overhead expenses and taxes). Then break that figure down into what you would need to make each month, a week, and a day. This will give you your daily labor rate.

To figure how much money you need to "gross" (gross income is how much you make before subtracting overhead expenses and taxes), take your daily labor rate, add in your average daily expenses, and multiply that number by 44 percent. (Experts estimate that overhead for a self-employed individual averages 44 percent of labor).

For example, a copywriter may want to charge $75-$95 per hour to cover overhead and time or may want to charge per project, instead. (Rates vary by geographical location: a writer in New York can charge more than one who lives in a rural area of the country because of demand and living expenses). Check this year's version of *Writer's Market* for ideas of how much to charge. This reference book is updated annually and publishes fee ranges for all types of writing services.

Save money on short-cuts

- Before you purchase new supplies or equipment, make sure you really need them. Impulse buying can put you into the red rather quickly.

- Recycle paper by re-feeding sheets through your printer, using the blank sides for rough drafts of your work. You can also cut the paper in half and staple it together for homemade "note pads."

- Purchase furniture and equipment at garage sales and auctions. If possible, find out if they are selling what you want and, if you can, look at it before the official sale/auction starts.

- Sometimes businesses throw away good usable equipment/furniture they no longer need. Just keep your eyes and ears open. Also, stay alert for news of firms leaving the area or closing departments. They are often sources for inexpensive office supplies.

Monitoring your money makes "cents"

If you're like most entrepreneurs, money management isn't at the top of your "favorites" list. However, it's one of the most important components of a stable business. Keeping track of expenses and knowing where every penny goes sounds miserly until you understand the sound economic principles behind it. So get a ledger, whether it's in electronic form or a book, and start recording your transactions!

Chapter 7 assignment: *Tax deductions and other money matters.*
(Check off and record the date when you accomplish each activity).

1. □ / date _____ Make a list of common tax-deductible items and post it in your office where you can see it as a daily reminder to keep track of everything for tax purposes.

2. □ / date _____ Get a large (at least 9x12) manila envelope and label it "business expenses and deductions" on the outside. Start putting all your receipts in this envelope.

3. □ / date _____ Put together a budget for equipment and supplies. If funds are limited, look in the newspaper for garage sales, auctions, business liquidations, etc.

4. □ / date _____ Research and start organizing a basic business plan.

5. □ / date _____ Establish a sound bookkeeping system, and keep track of income and expenses on a daily basis.

6. □ / date _____ Apply for a DBA license.

7. □ / date _____ Obtain a sales tax identification number (if applicable).

8. □ / date _____ Set up a business checking account.

9. □ / date _____ Investigate all avenues to set up a merchant account. Give yourself at least three days before signing up for merchant services.

‹‹NOTES››

CHAPTER 8

Making Medical Insurance More Affordable

"Seek not, my soul, the life of the immortals,
but enjoy to the full the resources that are within thy reach."
Pindar

Obtaining medical coverage is perhaps one of the biggest concerns for those who are self-employed. Just like everyone else, small business owners and their families need medical insurance but the skyrocketing costs are becoming prohibitive. And what about those who rarely visit the doctor, yet dare not go without coverage? Well, there is good news. It's called the Health Savings Account (HSA).

Signed into law by President George W. Bush on December 8, 2003, HSAs have helped make health coverage more affordable for millions of Americans. A Health Savings Account is a tax-exempt trust or custodial account covering qualifying medical expenses for those also enrolled in a high-deductible health insurance plan (HDHP).

There are no income limits and no earned income requirements to contribute to an HSA. Anyone is eligible for an HSA who is not covered by additional health insurance, other than the HDHP policy. (Exceptions are policies covering accidents, disability, dental care or long-term care).

Generally, a person is ineligible for an HSA if that individual, while covered under an HDHP, is also covered under a health plan (whether as an individual, spouse, or dependent) that is not an HDHP. These individuals cannot be enrolled in Medicare and cannot be claimed as a dependent on someone else's tax return.

The low-premium, high-deductible insurance policies connected with HSAs benefit individuals with low health care costs. Here's how it works: As a self-employed individual, you purchase health insurance with a high annual deductible and low premiums for your family. You use the policy savings to establish an HSA. Medical costs incurred by your family are paid out of funds from the investment account. Once the out-of-pocket deductible has been met, the insurance policy pays for additional medical care.

Following are the basic tenets of an HSA:

- Any individual who is covered by a high-deductible health plan may establish an HSA.

- Amounts contributed to an HSA belong to individuals and are completely portable.

- Every year, the money not spent stays in the account and gains interest, tax-free, just like an Individual Retirement Account (IRA). Unused amounts remain available for later years (unlike amounts in Flexible Spending Plans that are forfeited if not used by the end of the year).

- Funds distributed from the HSA are not taxed if they are used to pay qualifying medical expenses.

HSAs and how they work

The United States Treasury Department Web site summarizes information about Health Savings Accounts.

Advantages of HSAs

Security—Your high deductible insurance and HSA protect you against high or unexpected medical bills.

Affordability—You should be able to lower your health insurance premiums by switching to health insurance coverage with a higher deductible.

Flexibility—You can use the funds in your account to pay for current medical expenses, including expenses that your insurance may not cover, or save the money in your account for future needs, such as:

- Health insurance or medical expenses if unemployed
- Medical expenses after retirement (before Medicare)
- Out-of-pocket expenses when covered by Medicare
- Long-term care expenses and insurance

Savings—You can save the money in your account for future medical expenses and increase the worth of that account through investment earnings.

Control—You make all the decisions about:

- How much money to put into the account
- Whether to save the account for future expenses or pay current medical expenses
- Which medical expenses to pay from the account
- Which company will hold the account
- Whether to invest any of the money in the account
- Which investments to make

Portability—Accounts are completely portable, meaning you can keep your HSA even if you:

- Change jobs
- Change your medical coverage
- Move to another state
- Change your marital status

Ownership—Funds remain in the account from year to year, just like an IRA. There are no "use it or lose it" rules for HSAs.

Tax Savings—An HSA provides you triple tax savings.

- Tax deductions when you contribute to your account
- Tax-free earnings through investment
- Tax-free withdrawals for qualified medical expenses

High Deductible Health Plans (HDHPs)

Generally, this type of health insurance does not cover first dollar medical expenses. Federal law requires that the health insurance deductible be at least:

$1,050—Self-only coverage
$2,100—Family coverage

In addition, annual out-of-pocket expenses under the plan (including deductibles, co-pays, and co-insurance) cannot exceed:

$5,250*—Self-only coverage
$10,500*—Family coverage

In general, the deductible must apply to all medical expenses (including prescriptions) covered by the plan. However, plans can pay for "preventive care" services on a first-dollar basis (with or without a co-pay).

2006 amounts; adjusted annually for inflation.

Opening your HSA

Banks, credit unions, insurance companies and other financial institutions are permitted to be trustees or custodians of these accounts. If you cannot locate a local association that handles HSAs, check links under "Resources" at www.treasury.gov/offices/public-affairs/hsa/.

Make sure you are enrolled in a high deductible health plan (HDHP) that will qualify you to participate in a Health Savings Account, then contact your local insurance agent for information in setting up an HSA. You may also wish to consult with legal, medical, and tax professionals for advice pertaining to your specific circumstances.

Online health insurance information

There is strength in numbers. Joining trade associations or small business organizations, instead of going solo, could give you more affordable rates. Look before you leap: evaluate the benefits you really need before you shop around for coverage. Don't sign up for more than you need and this will help you cut costs. If you can afford to pay a higher deductible, it can often lower your monthly payments.

The National Association of Health Underwriters (NAHU) offers helpful guides containing valuable information on a variety of health insurance topics, including Health Savings Accounts. The following is excerpted from their Web site, as samples of content.

"Consumer Guide to Individual Health Insurance

Approximately five percent of Americans do not get their health insurance coverage through an employer or through a government program, but instead purchase private individual coverage. Individual coverage is regulated differently by each state which can have a tremendous impact on the individual health insurance products available to consumers in each state. This guide helps explain some of the nuances involved with purchasing private individual health insurance coverage.

"Consumer Guide to Continuation of Coverage

Millions of people who lose their group coverage due to a job change, divorce, job loss or other reason are able to keep their group coverage temporarily. There are several types of continuation coverage that individuals might be eligible for, depending on the past employment situation and state of residence. This guide provides information about continuation of coverage options, as well as the federal group-to-individual health insurance portability rights many people have.

"Consumer Guide to High-Risk Pools

For many people with serious pre-existing medical conditions, the prospect of finding individual insurance coverage outside of an employer group can be very daunting. However, most states have high-risk health insurance pools available, which can provide such individuals with access to affordable private coverage. These state high-risk pool programs are detailed in the NAHU Guide to High-Risk Pools."

For more information, please visit www.nahu.org.

Chapter 8 assignment: *More affordable health insurance.*
(Check off and record the date when you accomplish each activity).

1. ☐ / date _____ Get in touch with your local insurance agent and ask about Health Savings Accounts, as part of your medical insurance coverage portfolio.

2. ☐ / date _____ Enroll in a low-premium, high-deductible insurance policy.

3. ☐ / date _____ Check with your tax professional about your particular circumstances.

4. ☐ / date _____ Figure out how much you would like to contribute to your Health Savings Account.

5. ☐ / date _____ Ask your lending institution about setting up a Health Savings Account.

Time Management Tips

"Dost thou love life?
Then do not squander time,
for that is the stuff life is made of."
Benjamin Franklin

O ne of the hardest transitions many entrepreneurs face when going from a corporate environment to working independently is the lack of structure. You are responsible for determining your own schedule and for accomplishing jobs in a given amount of time. No one is there telling you what to do and when to do it, so diversions will present themselves. Discipline yourself and resist the urge for time-wasting activities like snacking in the kitchen, gabbing on the phone, and watching television.

Following are some helpful hints to help you stay on track:

- Start each day with a planning period of 10-30 minutes.

- Create a daily master task list, recording key tasks you'd like to accomplish for that day. (Schedule in personal time to help maintain balance).

- Set a time limit to accomplish a certain project.

- Break large projects into smaller, more manageable tasks.

- Work on the most complicated and detailed projects during your best concentration hours, whether in the morning or afternoon.

- Allow twice as much time as you think a task will take.

- File papers in labeled folders instead of stacks on your desk or on the floor. Scan documents and save them to a CD, to help further eliminate clutter.

Information management

As your business expands, you may find it convenient to keep electronic records of your customers, vendors, and other business contacts. Inexpensive database software packages, such as Goldmine®, will help you organize marketing activities and mailing lists, and keep track of transactions with current and potential customers.

Etiquette around the clock

It is vital you maintain a positive business image in all your transactions with the public. Punctuality is an asset. Be respectful of others' time. If you schedule a meeting with a client, be prompt! Taking time off for traveling? Make your clients aware of your availability and check e-mail and messages frequently to stay in touch.

Manage your time wisely

Keep going forward with your goal, even if you have to take baby steps. Perhaps you have to work your plans around a full-time job or other obligations. Only have 15 minutes to spare early in the morning or on a lunch break? The key is…DO SOMETHING! Following are a few suggestions to help you manage your time efficiently:

1. Determine how many hours per day or week you will devote to your business.

2. Set a regular schedule (two hours in the early morning before work; two hours after dinner; four hours on a Saturday, etc.).

3. As mentioned before, give yourself sub-deadlines in incremental time blocks: i.e., set aside a certain task that you will accomplish in a designated time frame, say between 10 a.m. and noon.

Success takes time...take time for success!

It takes time to build a solid business. If you are working fulltime, start small and steadily grow from there. This approach will save your sanity. Additionally, you will be able to see if there is a true market for what you are offering and if it is something you will enjoy doing on a long-term basis. Give yourself three-to-six months to prepare the foundation. Time will be on your side, if you manage it wisely!

Chapter 9 assignment: *Time management tips.*

(Check off and record the date when you accomplish each activity).

Do the following daily, as a regular part of your business schedule.

1. ☐ / date _____ Start the day with a planning period of 10-30 minutes.

2. ☐ / date _____ Create a daily master task list, recording key tasks you'd like to accomplish for that day. (Schedule in personal time to help maintain balance).

3. ☐ / date _____File papers in labeled folders instead of stacks on your desk or on the floor.

4. ☐ / date _____ Break large projects into more manageable projects.

5. ☐ / date _____ Determine how many hours per day or week you will devote to your business.

6. ☐ / date _____ Set a regular schedule (two hours in the early morning before work; two hours after dinner; four hours on a Saturday, etc.).

CHAPTER 10

Pull It All Together

"Whatever you are by nature, keep to it;
never desert your line of talent.
Be what nature intended you for and you will succeed."
Sydney Smith

Look at the businesses flourishing in your community. Each one began as an idea—a mere figment of someone's imagination. That was the seed. Then someone had to nourish the seed. Your business idea must be cultivated, as well, with a positive outlook and persistence. Never entertain thoughts of defeat—even in the face of opposition and obstacles. In his motivational book *The Power of Intention*, Dr. Wayne W. Dyer observes:

> "There's a silent something within that intends you to express yourself…That silent inner knowing will never leave you alone. You may try to ignore it and pretend it doesn't exist, but in honest, alone moments of contemplative communion with yourself, you sense the emptiness waiting for you to fill it with your music. It wants you to take the risks involved, and to ignore your ego and the egos of others who tell you that an easier, safer, or more secure path is best for you.

> "…It's about sharing yourself in a creative, loving way using the skills and interest that are inherently part of you. It can involve any activity: dancing, writing, healing, gardening, cooking, parenting, teaching, composing, singing, surfing—whatever. There's no limit to this list…If the activities on this list are in

service to others, you feel the bliss of purposeful living, while paradoxically attracting more of what you'd like to have in your life."

And Oprah Winfrey, a model of success who overcame adversities thrust upon her at an early age, says,

"The whole point of being alive is to evolve into the complete person you were intended to be. I believe you can only do this when you stop long enough to hear the whisper you might have drowned out, that small voice compelling you toward the kind of work you'd be willing to do even if you weren't paid. Once you tune out the noise of your life and hear that call, you face the biggest challenge of all: to find the courage to seek out your big dream, regardless of what anyone else says or thinks."

Remember to visualize yourself as already doing that which you would like to do. Envision the end result, as if you've already achieved your goal, and the details will fall into place to make it happen.

To help you "pull it all together," here is a quick review of the success formula. Remember to copy the worksheets, then check off each step as you accomplish it, for best results.

1. *Start with a winning attitude.* The maxim by Henry Ford, quoted earlier, sums it up pretty well: "Think you can; think you can't—either way you're right."

2. *Do you what you enjoy.* Dedicate your efforts in an area that drives your passions and interests. Match your skills with a way you can be of service to others, and a service for which they would be willing to pay. You'll find that a steady income will be the successful by-product of your excellent service and hard work.

3. *Conduct your market research.* Learn your potential customers' attitudes, preferences, age group and as much as possible about them. As stated before, this will help you tailor your product or service to their wants and needs. So do your homework!

4. *Establish your business structure and identity.* Study the various types of business organizations and select the one that aligns with your particular endeavor, whether it is a sole proprietorship or more formal entity.

5. *Choose your office location.* This will be determined by your budget and type of business, as well as your lifestyle. Remember to begin with as low overhead as possible and then expand to a different location as your enterprise grows.

6. *Use savvy advertising and marketing techniques.* The only way to attract customers is to let them know your business exists. The next step is to tell them what you offer and how it can help them be richer, smarter, slimmer, save time, make money, grow better gardens, organize their lives, get better jobs, etc. Select the type of advertising that best suits your business budget.

7. *Be aware of tax deductions and other important money matters.* Keep careful records of all receipts and financial transactions to maximize your income and minimize your tax liabilities. A separate business checking account will help you organize and keep everything straight.

8. *Develop a Health Savings Account (HSA).* Read carefully the advantages of, qualifications for, and restrictions of HSAs. Check with a qualified insurance agent or financial planner for more information.

9. *Manage and organize your time.* Remember to organize your workday, keep records/papers in file folders and electronic backups on CDs. Set reasonable deadlines and don't become discouraged. It takes several months to get a new business up and running and to establish a solid customer base. So don't quit your day job right away!

Support through associations

It's important to stay in touch with other like-minded entrepreneurs because there is strength in numbers. As mentioned in Chapter 6, joining your local Chamber of Commerce is a good way to find networking contacts and enjoy vital emotional support. Even though you have to pay membership fees and there may be other lesser miscellaneous costs, it will be worth it. Remember that all expenses associated with your business are tax deductible! Sometimes Chambers offer group benefits, similar to what you would receive from an employer. Most of them regularly sponsor luncheons, speakers, and events that keep you mentally focused on your business. And who knows…you may even meet some businesspeople with ventures complementary to your own. In that case, consider teaming up efforts and helping each other!

Get ready; get organized; get started!

The most difficult part about succeeding in a new business is taking the first step. So don't waste any more time! Discipline is the key to getting started. Determine exactly what you want and then work toward it. You can wish and dream all you want, but unless you act, you will never reach your goal.

Before this day is over, sit down at your desk or kitchen table with a notebook and pen. Instead of watching TV, concentrate and brainstorm about your new pursuit: what you would like to do and how you can turn it into a viable business. Write down any and all ideas that come to you. You will find that one idea will lead to another. Print off the worksheet pages in this book and put them where you can see them every day. Check off and record the date you accomplish each activity. Doing so will help you stay on course and reach your goals.

Also, stay flexible. If something doesn't work out quite the way you envisioned, don't be afraid to try something new. This book was originally intended solely as a seminar/workshop curriculum. However, I expanded it into a book format, feeling the information could reach additional people that way. So here it is. And it all began as a "figment of my imagination!"

Chapter 10: Final assignment: *Master worksheet (review).*
Copy this section and record your progress. Put it in an area where you can see it every day to remind you of your goals. Remember to check off and record the date when you accomplish each activity!

Start with a winning attitude.

1. □ / date _____ Go to your public library or a local well-stocked bookstore with a notepad and pen. Review magazines such as *Entrepreneur Magazine*, *Home Business Magazine*, and others like them. Then take time to read key articles that capture your interest. Make notes.

2. □ / date _____ Seek out motivational books like *The Power of Intention*, *The Millionaire Mind*, *Think & Grow Rich*, and others like them. Review the chapter headings, and make notes.

3. □ / date _____ Invest in yourself and your business by purchasing (or at least checking out of the library) one or more magazines and books in this topic area.

4. □ / date _____ Pray/meditate about your new venture.

5. □ / date _____ Write down five positive statements (commonly called "affirmations") regarding your business goal. Write them down as if you have already achieved them and review them twice a day. Examples are:

    •   I am a successful (fill in the blank) computer training consultant, Web site designer, resumé writer, bookkeeper, etc.

    •   I am making (fill in the blank) $1,000 a month, $3,000 a month, $5,000 a month, etc.

    •   I am happy and organized.

    •   I love serving and helping others achieve their dreams.

    •   I find time to build my business.

Choose what you enjoy.

6. □ / date _____ Ask someone close to you (a friend or relative) for an objective opinion of where they feel your talents and strengths lie.

7. □ / date _____ Explore ideas at your local bookstore or library by reviewing magazines and books directed to home businesses and entrepreneurs. You will find fascinating success stories of other business-builders and who knows…these stories may spark a fire of interest in areas you had not previously considered!

8. □ / date _____ Review your three favorite hobbies, skills or talents.

_____

_____

_____

_____

9. □ / date _____ Write down the one you think you could develop into a business.

_____

_____

10. □ / date _____ List a way you could meet a market need with this skill (i.e., teach a class, fix something, provide a service, etc.).

_____

_____

_____

_____

_____

_____

Conduct your market research

11. □ / date _____ Develop a survey questionnaire about your product or service and distribute it to friends and acquaintances that you think may fit into your target market.

12. □ / date _____ Identify direct competitors in your local area.

13. □ / date _____ What are their market niches? (Low prices and quality goods?).

14. □ / date _____ Examine competitor marketing tactics. (Soft sell? Aggressive hard-sell?) Or gimmicky like the Southern California car dealer who brought out exotic animals at different times on his television commercials and introduced each as his dog Spot? This was a very unusual attention-grabber. Unusual, but effective!

15. □ / date _____ Study your favorite tactics you feel have worked best with customers and make note of advertising ploys you do not like.

16. □ / date _____ Start a file of niche marketing techniques and examples you would like to emulate, as well as those you would like to avoid.

17. □ / date _____ Identify your market niche—that small, unique segment of consumers who need a specific product or service.

18. □ / date _____ Identify key areas that will set you apart from the competition and use these as marketing points in your advertising.

Your business structure and identity

19. □ / date _____ Decide what type of business structure you will work under (i.e., sole proprietorship, partnership, corporation, "S" corporation, or LLC).

20. □ / date _____ Select your business name. Remember, it should reflect the type of product or service you offer.

21. □ / date ____ Make sure your business name is available and unregistered.

22. □ / date ____ Develop a slogan or tagline that incorporates your company's mission statement.

23. □ / date ____ Create a memorable logo.

Selecting your office space

24. □ / date ____ Describe where your ideal office will be held (at home or away from home) and the size of the space.

_____

_____

_____

25. □ / date ____ Describe how you will furnish your office.

_____

_____

_____

26. □ / date ____ Look at your office from your potential client's point of view and make note of ideas for improvement.

_____

_____

_____

27. □ / date ____ Make a list of basic equipment you will need.

_____

_____

_____

28. ☐ / date _____ From this chapter, list your three favorite reasons for becoming self-employed (i.e., financial freedom, greater flexibility of time, security, etc.).

_____

_____

_____

_____

Advertising and marketing

29. ☐ / date _____ Prepare an advertising budget. Make a list and corresponding costs of items such as business cards, stationery, promotional brochures, printing costs, and advertising fees.

30. ☐ / date _____ Figure out pricing for your products or services.

31. ☐ / date _____ Develop your advertising campaign first by deciding on your promotional and advertising literature.

32. ☐ / date _____ Determine how you will reach the largest segment of your target customers.

33. ☐ / date _____ Set dates to accomplish each advertising strategy (i.e., classified ads, flyers, radio ads, etc.) and mark them on your calendar.

Tax deductions and other money matters

34. ☐ / date _____ Make a list of common tax-deductible items and post it in your office where you can see it daily to remind yourself to keep track of everything for tax purposes.

35. ☐ / date _____ Get a large (at least 9x12) manila envelope and label it "business expenses and deductions" on the outside. Start putting all your receipts in this envelope.

36. □ / date _____ Put together a budget for equipment and supplies. If funds are limited, look in the newspaper for garage sales, auctions, business liquidations, etc.

37. □ / date _____ Research and start organizing a basic business plan.

38. □ / date _____ Establish a sound bookkeeping system, and keep track of income and expenses on a daily basis.

39. □ / date _____ Apply for a DBA license.

40. □ / date _____ Obtain a sales tax identification number (if applicable).

41. □ / date _____ Set up a business checking account.

42. □ / date _____ Investigate all avenues to set up a merchant account. Give yourself at least three days before signing up for merchant services

More affordable health insurance

43. □ / date _____ Get in touch with your local insurance agent and ask about Health Savings Accounts, as part of your medical insurance coverage portfolio.

44. □ / date _____ Enroll in a low-premium, high-deductible insurance policy.

45. □ / date _____ Check with your tax professional about your particular circumstances.

46. □ / date _____ Figure out how much you would like to contribute to your Health Savings Account.

47. □ / date _____ Ask your lending institution about setting up an HSA.

Time management tips

Do the following daily, as a regular part of your business schedule.

48. □ / date _____ Start the day with a planning period of 10-30 minutes.

49. □ / date _____ Create a daily master task list, recording key tasks you'd like to accomplish for that day. (Schedule in personal time to help maintain balance).

50. □ / date _____File papers in labeled folders instead of stacks on your desk.

51. □ / date _____ Break large projects into more manageable projects.

52. □ / date _____ Determine how many hours per day or week you will devote to your business.

53. □ / date _____ Set a regular schedule (two hours in the early morning before work; two hours after dinner; four hours on a Saturday, etc.).

‹‹NOTES››

Suggested Reading

Books

- *The Power of Intention* by Dr. Wayne W. Dyer
- *Guerrilla Marketing: Secrets for Making Big Profits From Your Small Business* by Jay Conrad Levinson
- *Moneymaking Moms: How Work at Home Can Work for You* by Caroline Hill and Tanya Wallace
- *6 Steps to Free Publicity and Dozens of Other Ways to Win Free Media Attention For You or Your Business* by Marcia Yudkin
- *The Successful Business Organizer* by Rhonda M. Abrams
- *Start Your Own Business: The Only Start-Up Book You'll Ever Need* by Rieva Lesonsky
- *Why Aren't You Your Own Boss: Leaping Over the Obstacles That Stand Between You and Your Dream* by Paul Edwards, Sarah Edwards, Peter Economy
- *The Millionaire Mind* by Thomas J. Stanley, Ph.D
- *Think & Grow Rich* by Napoleon Hill
- *You Can Work Your Own Miracles* by Napoleon Hill
- *The Power of Your Subconscious Mind* by Dr. Joseph Murphy
- *The Magic of Believing* by Claude M. Bristol
- *Do What You Love; The Money Will Follow* by Marsha Sinetar

Magazines and Web sites

- Entrepreneur Magazine (www.entrepreneur.com)
- Home Business Magazine (www.homebusinessmag.com)
- Inc. Magazine (www.inc.com)

About the Author

Debbie Barwick forged the foundation for her vocation early in life. An avid reader at a tender age, she enjoyed creating stories and poetry and remembers her third-grade teacher reading her compositions to her young classmates. Debbie served as editor of her junior high school paper and later launched a hobby of freelancing for city newspapers with the advent of a column titled "You and Your Dollar."

Her passion for writing and her curiosity about a wide variety of subjects propelled her into a solid journalism career. While working as a fulltime corporate copywriter, she authored books, one-act plays, and newspaper articles, besides producing a variety of other freelance work. Eventually, she set up shop with her own professional freelance copywriting service. Through all this experience, she studied and learned firsthand the basic principles of starting and maintaining a successful business.

Over the years, Debbie met many people with the desire to strike out on their own but lacked the knowledge of how or where to begin. At the same time, she was intrigued by discovering numerous entrepreneurs with businesses revolving around their unique talents and experience. These people seemed to be the happiest, doing what they loved. Investigating further, she discovered they also commonly exhibited two fundamental characteristics: persistence and business savvy. After years of studying and exploring ways people could create revenue-generating enterprises centered around their passions, "Turn Your Talents Into Gold" was born.

A member of the Society of Professional Journalists, Debbie emphasizes, "I love to research and write information that will help people better their lives."

Printed in Great Britain
by Amazon.co.uk, Ltd.,
Marston Gate.